THE SCIENCE BEHIND

Weather

Darlene Stille

Raintree

www.raintreepublishers.co.uk
Visit our website to find out
more information about
Raintree books.

To order:
☎ Phone 0845 6044371
🖷 Fax +44 (0) 1865 312263
🖳 Email myorders@raintreepublishers.co.uk

Customers from outside the UK please telephone +44 1865 312262

Edited by Megan Cotugno and Laura Knowles
Designed by Richard Parker
Picture research by Mica Brancic
Original Illustrations © Capstone Global Library
    Ltd 2012
Illustrations by Oxford Designers & Illustrators
Originated by Capstone Global Library Ltd
Printed and bound in China by Leo Paper
    Products Ltd

ISBN 978 1 406 23400 8 (hardback)
15 14 13 12 11
10 9 8 7 6 5 4 3 2 1

ISBN 978 1 406 23406 0 (paperback)
17 16 15 14 13
10 9 8 7 6 5 4 3 2 1

British Library Cataloguing in Publication Data
Stille, Darlene R.
The science behind weather.
551.6-dc22
A full catalogue record for this book is available
from the British Library.

Acknowledgements
We would like to thank the following for
permission to reproduce photographs: Alamy,
p. **22** (© Michael Dwyer); Getty Images p. **24**
(Photodisc/Kim Steele); NASA p. **18** (MODIS Rapid
Response Team); Photolibrary p. **21** (Oxford
Scientific (OSF)/Warren Faidley); Science Photo
Library p. **7** (NASA); Shutterstock pp. **4** (© Josef
Bosak), **5** (© Gemphotography), **8** (© Natalia
Macheda), **9** (© Leonid_tit), **10** (© Smit), **13**
(© Vesilvio), **14** (© Fedorov Oleksiy), **17** (© SVLuma).

Cover photograph of a summer storm beginning
with lightning reproduced with permission of
Shutterstock/© Leonid_tit.

We would like to thank David Crowther and Nancy
Harris for their invaluable help in the preparation
of this book.

Every effort has been made to contact copyright
holders of any material reproduced in this book.
Any omissions will be rectified in subsequent
printings if notice is given to the publisher.

Contents

Look for these boxes:

Stay safe
These boxes tell you how to keep yourself and your friends safe from harm.

In your day
These boxes show you how science is a part of your daily life.

Measure up!
These boxes give you some fun facts and figures to think about.

Some words appear in bold, **like this**. You can find out what they mean by looking at the green bar at the bottom of the page or in the glossary.

What's it like outside?

Raindrops run down the windowpane. **Sunlight** shines on the pavement. It could be sunny or cloudy today. It might be raining or snowing outside. Will you go for a walk or play indoors? Will you wear a coat and gloves? Will you take an umbrella to school? What you can do and what you will wear all depends on the weather.

Playing on the beach is fun on a warm, sunny day.

sunlight   light that comes from the Sun

On rainy days you may have to stay indoors and read or play a game.

Stay safe

You need to dress warmly on cold days when the **wind** is blowing. Wind makes the temperature outdoors feel colder. Extreme cold can cause **frostbite**, which means parts of your body freeze. Fingers and toes that are not inside warm gloves or boots can become frostbitten.

wind   moving air
frostbite   injury to part of the body because of freezing cold temperature

What is weather?

Weather is what is happening in the air around you and above you. The air goes high up into the sky. The air is **gas** that surrounds Earth like a blanket. Air can feel warm or cold. This blanket of air is called the **atmosphere**.

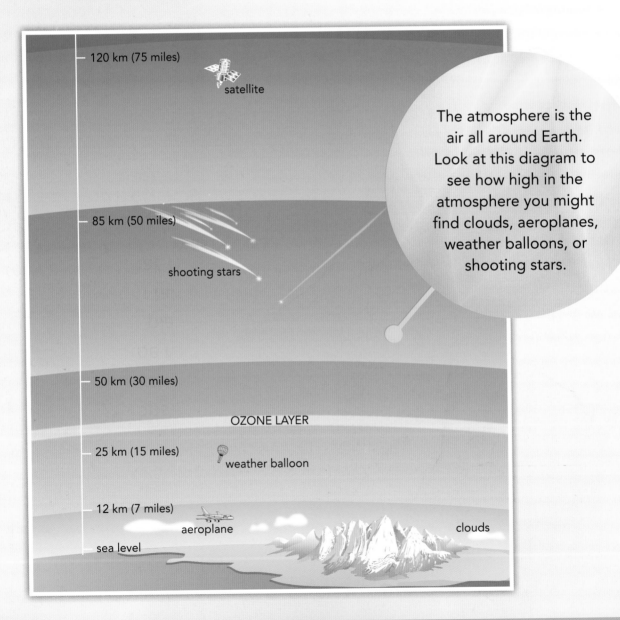

120 km (75 miles)

satellite

The atmosphere is the air all around Earth. Look at this diagram to see how high in the atmosphere you might find clouds, aeroplanes, weather balloons, or shooting stars.

85 km (50 miles)

shooting stars

50 km (30 miles)

OZONE LAYER

25 km (15 miles)

weather balloon

12 km (7 miles)

aeroplane   clouds

sea level

---

gas   vapour that is not a liquid or a solid

You cannot see the atmosphere. You can see weather happening in the atmosphere. You can see clouds. Rain and snow fall from clouds in the atmosphere.

The **wind** blows in the atmosphere. Wind is moving air. You cannot see air, but you can feel it when the wind blows.

Scientists use special balloons to study the atmosphere. These weather balloons measure the temperature and how much water is in the atmosphere.

Measure up

How many days are sunny where you live? Find out! Make notes on a wall calendar. Each day, write on the calendar whether the weather was sunny, cloudy, snowy, or rainy. After a month, count up how many days had each kind of weather.

atmosphere   air, made of gases, that surrounds Earth

Weather changes

The weather can change from day to day and month to month. One day can be cool and cloudy, and the next can be hot and sunny. Weather is what happens outdoors in a certain place.

The weather at the North Pole is cold. Some days are colder than others. The weather at the **equator** is warm. The equator is an imaginary line around the middle of Earth.

Most places near the equator have a wet, warm climate. Plants grow all the year round.

equator   imaginary line around the middle of Earth

Snow falls near the North Pole, or during the cold winter in places with four seasons.

Weather and climate

The kind of weather that a place has year after year is called **climate**. The North Pole has a cold climate. The equator has a warm climate. Places in between have hot summers and cold winters. These places have climates with four seasons – spring, summer, autumn, and winter.

Stay safe

It is fun to play in the sun, but the sun can burn your skin. When you are in the sun, wear a hat and use sunscreen.

climate   the kind of weather that a place has year after year

Seasons and weather

Do you live in a place with four seasons? In the warm spring, flowers start to bloom. In the hot summer, the days are long and sunny. In the cool autumn, trees turn red and gold. In the cold winter, there can be enough snow to build a snowman.

Many trees have buds in spring, green leaves in summer, red or gold leaves in autumn, and bare branches in winter.

How Earth moves

Earth turns on an imaginary "stick" called an **axis**. Earth turns around on its axis once every 24-hour day. It is daytime on the side facing the Sun. It is night on the other side.

axis   imaginary stick through the centre of the Earth

Earth also tilts on its axis. The tilt causes four seasons in some places. The tilted Earth goes around the Sun once a year. Because of Earth's tilt, the Sun warms different parts of Earth during a year.

Where the Sun shines on Earth, it is daytime. Where Earth is in shadow, it is night. Some places on Earth have four seasons because Earth tilts as it goes around the Sun.

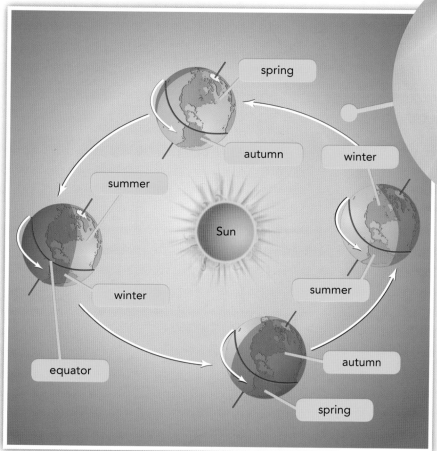

In your day

Watch how a spinning top tilts as it spins. The top spins around its axis. Earth spins a lot like a spinning top.

Cloud watching

Look at clouds. Clouds can be puffy, long and thin, flat, or as tall as mountains.

Cirrus clouds are white, thin, and feathery

Cumulonimbus clouds are tall and thick

Cumulus clouds are white and puffy

Stratus clouds blanket the sky

How clouds form

Clouds form from water in the air. Small beads of water, called **water droplets**, form around tiny bits of dust or smoke. The droplets are light enough to float in air. Billions of droplets come together to make a cloud. If it is cold enough, the droplets freeze into tiny **ice crystals**.

water droplet   very small amount of water
ice crystal   tiny speck of ice

Rain or snow

Water droplets in clouds grow into raindrops. Ice crystals stick to one another and become snowflakes. Raindrops and snowflakes fall as rain or snow.

Drought

Sometimes there are no clouds in the sky. It does not rain or snow for a long time. The soil dries out and plants die. A time with no rain is called a **drought**.

When there is a drought, fields of corn are dried out.

In your day

When you have a hot shower, your bathroom mirror "fogs up". **Fog** outdoors forms in the same way. Fog is like a cloud that touches the ground. When warm, "wet" air touches the ground (or your mirror), fog forms.

drought   time when there is little or no rain or snow
fog   thick cloud lying on the ground that is difficult to see through

13

Thunderstorms

Lightning flashes! Thunder rumbles. Thunder and lightning are signs that a thunderstorm is on its way.

This is a thunderstorm cloud.

Special type of cloud

Thunderstorms come from a special type of cloud called a cumulonimbus cloud. These clouds are huge. They can be 64 kilometres (40 miles) wide. They tower up into the **atmosphere** as high as 16 kilometres (10 miles).

Thunderstorm clouds have flat tops. A point sticks forward from the top like the front of a ship.

What happens during a thunderstorm?

Heavy rain falls and strong **winds** blow. Sometimes balls of ice called **hail** fall.

Thunderstorms can be dangerous. The lightning can hit trees, buildings, and people. The heavy rain can cause floods. The winds can blow down trees.

Stay safe

Protect yourself from lightning. Stay indoors during a thunderstorm and keep away from windows. Stay out of water and never stand under a tree, which could be hit by lightning.

hail   balls of ice that sometimes fall during a thunderstorm

Blizzards

Blizzards are big storms that strike in winter. They drop snow instead of rain.

What happens during a blizzard?

Lots of snow falls during a blizzard. The snow falls so fast and thick that you cannot see where you are. Strong **winds** blow at speeds from 56 to more than 72 kilometres (35 to more than 45 miles) per hour. The wind blows the snow into big piles called **snowdrifts**. Cars and lorries can be buried in snowdrifts.

The temperature falls very low, and the air gets very cold. The temperature can drop to -12 °Celsius (10 °Fahrenheit) or below.

Stay safe

When you travel in a car during winter weather, take some emergency supplies. You might get stuck in a blizzard. Bring water to drink, snack bars to eat, and blankets to keep you warm. Bringing a torch is also a good idea.

snowdrift   snow that is blown by wind into big piles

A large amount of snow stops people from travelling.

What causes blizzards?

Cold air moves in from the polar regions. A blizzard forms where the cold air meets warm air.

Big winds: hurricanes

Some of the worst weather is caused by **winds** that swirl. Winds that blow in a big circle cause hurricanes.

How hurricanes form

A hurricane forms over warm ocean water. It begins as a smaller storm. Slowly, the wind gathers speed. When the wind swirls at more than 119 kilometres (74 miles) per hour, the storm is a hurricane.

The winds blow hurricane clouds into a doughnut-shaped ring. In the centre of the ring is a calm, clear area called the **eye of the hurricane**.

The swirling winds of a hurricane move across the ocean. In the centre is the eye of the hurricane.

How hurricanes move

Hurricanes move across the ocean. They can travel as far as 6,400 kilometres (4,000 miles) for as long as two weeks. Hurricanes often move towards land. Big waves as well as strong winds cause death and destruction.

Stay safe

Weather services try to tell where a hurricane will hit land. They send out warnings to people in the area. Sometimes, they ask people to **evacuate**, or leave their homes.

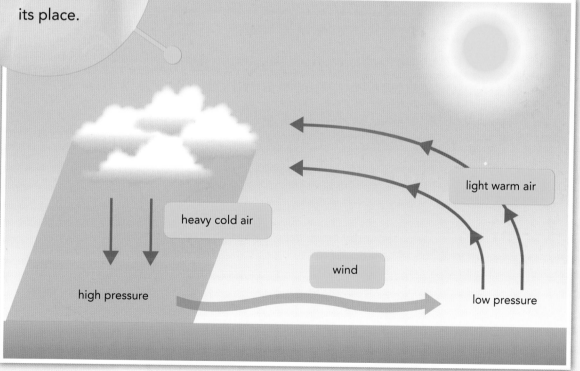

This diagram shows how wind forms. As warm air rises, cold air rushes in to take its place.

heavy cold air

light warm air

wind

high pressure

low pressure

evacuate leave an area

Twisting tornadoes

Tornadoes are rapidly spinning tubes of air. **Wind** makes the air spin. Tornadoes are shaped like a **funnel**.

Whirling danger

Tornadoes form inside thunderstorms. The funnel suddenly drops down from the cloud and touches the ground.

Tornadoes are like monstrous vacuum cleaners. The whirling winds in the funnel are strong enough to suck up cars, buildings, people, and animals. A big tornado can flatten a town in just a few minutes.

Funnels big and small

The wind in a funnel cloud can whirl at more than 420 kilometres (260 miles) per hour. Most tornadoes cause damage in a strip less than 500 metres (1,600 feet) wide. The biggest tornadoes can tear up a strip more than 1.6 kilometres (1 mile) wide.

Stay safe

During a tornado watch, people watch the sky for funnel clouds. If one is spotted, a tornado warning goes out. Then people go into a basement or another safe place underground until the tornado has blown away.

funnel   tube that is wide at the top and narrow at the bottom

This is the funnel cloud of a tornado that has dropped down from a thunderstorm.

An eye on the weather

Weather **forecasters** predict what the weather will be like. How do they know? How can they tell when it is raining far away?

Weather stations

Many countries have thousands of **weather stations** all over the world. Some are on land. Some float on the ocean. The countries share information.

This weather station is floating on the ocean.

forecaster   person who predicts what the weather will be like in the next few days
weather station   place that collects information about weather

Radar stations look for storms. Radar tracks how a storm is moving.

From space

Spacecraft called **satellites** watch the weather from space. Cameras and other instruments send information back to Earth.

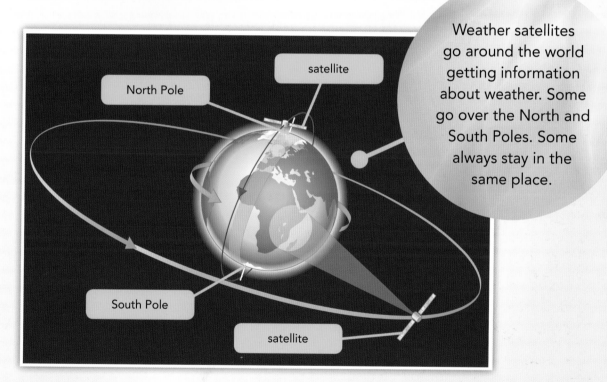

satellite

North Pole

Weather satellites go around the world getting information about weather. Some go over the North and South Poles. Some always stay in the same place.

South Pole

satellite

Instruments at these stations tell us what the weather is doing. Thermometers take the air temperature. Weather vanes show how the **wind** is blowing. Rain gauges measure how much rain or snow is falling. Another instrument tracks wind speed.

radar   instrument that sends out radio waves to find storms
satellite device that flies high above Earth and sends and receives
               information to and from Earth

23

The weather forecast

Weather **forecasters** use information from **satellites**, **radar**, and **weather stations**. The information helps them forecast, or predict, what the weather will be.

Other scientists use some of this information to study the **atmosphere**. It is growing warmer. The warming could cause Earth's **climate** to change, ice caps to melt, and flooding. Many scientists think that **pollution** is making the atmosphere warmer.

Computers make sense of weather information from instruments all over the world and in space.

pollution harmful substances that spoil a place and can harm living things
symbol mark or sign that stands for something

Weather forecasters also put weather information into powerful computers. The computers use maths to make a kind of model of the weather. The forecasters use the **computer models** to help make a forecast.

TV weather forecasts

The TV weather forecasters stand by a big map. Lines and arrows on the map are **symbols** that show what the weather might be like. Just think how many scientific instruments in space and around the world help you decide whether to wear a jumper or take an umbrella to school.

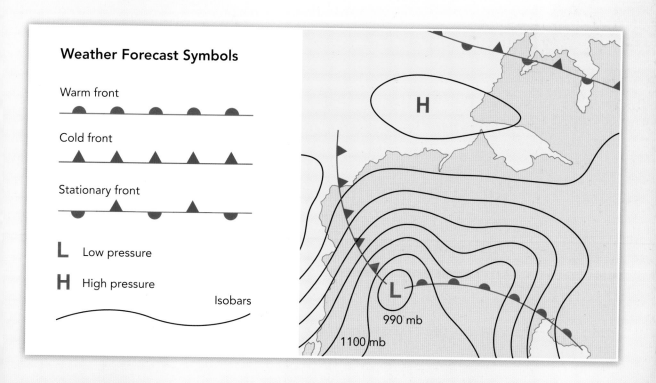

Weather Forecast Symbols

Warm front

Cold front

Stationary front

L   Low pressure

H   High pressure

Isobars

H

L

990 mb

1100 mb

Try it yourself

Making a rain gauge

What you need

- clear, plastic 2-litre bottle
- duct tape
- ruler
- permanent marker
- small marbles or stones

What to do

1. Ask an adult to help you cut the top off the plastic bottle.

2. Cover the sharp edges with duct tape.

3. Use a ruler and permanent marker to make a scale of horizontal lines on the bottom part of the bottle. You will use this scale for measuring. The lines should start 5 centimetres above the bottom. They should end 5 centimetres from the top.

plastic bottle

duct tape

ruler

scale

Each line must be separated by a 2-centimetre space.

4. Place the marbles or stones in the bottom of the bottle to hold it steady.

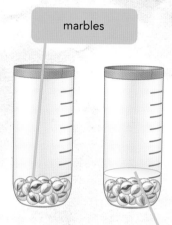

marbles

5. Fill the bottle with water up to the first line above the bottom.

6. Take the top part cut from the bottle and turn it upside down. Place it inside the bottom part of the bottle to form a **funnel**.

water

7. Take your rain gauge outside.

8. After it rains, check to see how many centimetres of water are in your rain gauge, above the first bottom line.

Caution

During times when there is little rainfall, the water in your gauge above the stones or marbles might evaporate (dry out). Be sure the bottle is filled to the first line, especially when rain is forecast.

Glossary

atmosphere air, made of gases, that surrounds Earth

axis imaginary stick through the centre of Earth

climate the kind of weather that a place has year after year

computer model computer program that stands for something in real life, such as wind and rain

drought time when there is little or no rain or snow

equator imaginary line around the middle of Earth

evacuate leave an area

eye of the hurricane calm, centre part of a hurricane

forecaster person who predicts what the weather will be like in the next few days

frostbite injury to part of the body because of freezing cold temperature

funnel tube that is wide at the top and narrow at the bottom

gas vapour that is not a liquid or a solid

hail balls of ice that sometimes fall during a thunderstorm

ice crystal tiny speck of ice

pollution harmful substances that spoil a place and can harm living things

radar instrument that sends out radio waves to find storms

satellite device that flies high above Earth and sends and receives information to and from Earth

snowdrift snow that is blown by wind into big piles

sunlight light that comes from the Sun

symbol mark or sign that stands for something

water droplet very small amount of water

weather station place that collects information about weather

wind moving air

Find out more

Use these resources to find more fun and useful information about the science behind weather.

Books

Blizzard (Wild Weather), Catherine Chambers (Heinemann Library, 2008)

Heat Wave (Wild Weather), Catherine Chambers (Heinemann Library, 2008)

How Does a Cloud Become a Thunderstorm? (How Does It Happen?), Mike Graf (Raintree, 2009)

Sunshine and Clouds (Measuring the Weather), Alan Rodgers and Angella Streluk (Heinemann Library, 2007)

Tornado (Wild Weather), Catherine Chambers (Heinemann Library, 2008)

Weather (Eyewitness Project Books), (Dorling Kindersley, 2008)

Websites

www.edheads.org/activities/weather
Visit this website to learn how to report and predict the weather with an animated weather forecaster.

www.metoffice.gov.uk/education/kids
The Met Office website has lots of games and activities to help you learn more about the weather.

www.scholastic.com/kids/weather
Control the weather using the interactive tools on this website.

**www.sciencemuseum.org.uk/onlinestuff/stories/
    heavy_weather.aspx**
Visit the Science Museum website to find out more about wild weather!

www.weatherwizkids.com
Learn more about the way weather works from a real meteorologist on this great website.

Index